D0091515

Compass Roses and Directions

by
Jennifer M. Besel

Consulting editor:
Gail Saunders-Smith, PhD

Consultant:
Dr. Sarah E. Battersby
Department of Geography
University of South Carolina

CAPSTONE PRESS
a capstone imprint

Pebble Books are published by Capstone Press,
1710 Roe Crest Drive, North Mankato, Minnesota 56003
www.capstonepub.com

Library of Congress Cataloging-in-Publication Data
Besel, Jennifer M.
Compass roses and directions / by Jennifer M. Besel.
p. cm.—(Pebble Books. Maps)
Includes bibliographical references and index.
Summary: "Simple text with full-color photos and illustrations provide basic
information about compass roses and map directions"—Provided by publisher.
ISBN 978-1-4765-3084-0 (library binding)—ISBN 978-1-4765-3506-7 (ebook pdf)—
ISBN 978-1-4765-3524-1 (paperback)
1. Cardinal points—Juvenile literature. 2. Maps—Symbols—Juvenile literature. I.
Title.
G108.5.C3B47 2014
912.01'48—dc23   2012046449

Editorial Credits
Gene Bentdahl, designer; Kathy McColley, production specialist; Sarah Schuette,
photo stylist; Marcy Morin, scheduler

Photo Credits
Capstone: 7, 9 (front); Capstone Studio: Karon Dubke, cover, 1, 5, 9 (back), 11, 13, 15,
17, 19, 21

Note to Parents and Teachers

The Maps set supports social studies standards related to people, places, and
environments. This book describes and illustrates compass roses and map directions.
The images support early readers in understanding the text. The repetition of words
and phrases helps early readers learn new words. This book also introduces early
readers to subject-specific vocabulary words, which are defined in the Glossary
section. Early readers may need assistance to read some words and to use the Table
of Contents, Glossary, Read More, Internet Sites, and Index sections of the book.

Printed in the United States of America in North Mankato, Minnesota.
032013   007223CGF13

Table of Contents

Which Way?. 4
Getting Directions 8
Compasses. 14
Using Map Tools. 16

Glossary 22
Read More 23
Internet Sites. 23
Critical Thinking Using the Common Core. . . 24
Index 24

Which Way?

Have you ever been lost?

A map is a great tool

to help you find your way.

On a map you can see
roads or buildings.

Maps show which direction
one place is from another.

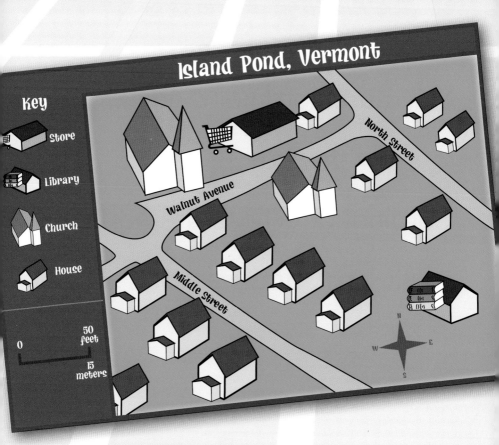

Island Pond, Vermont

Key

Store

Library

Church

House

0   50 feet

15 meters

Walnut Avenue

North Street

Middle Street

N
W   E
S

Getting Directions

Maps use cardinal directions to show the way.

Cardinal directions are north, south, east, and west.

North

West ⟷ East

South

Village ▪   ▪ Fishing Bridge

The compass rose shows which way is north, south, east, or west on the map.

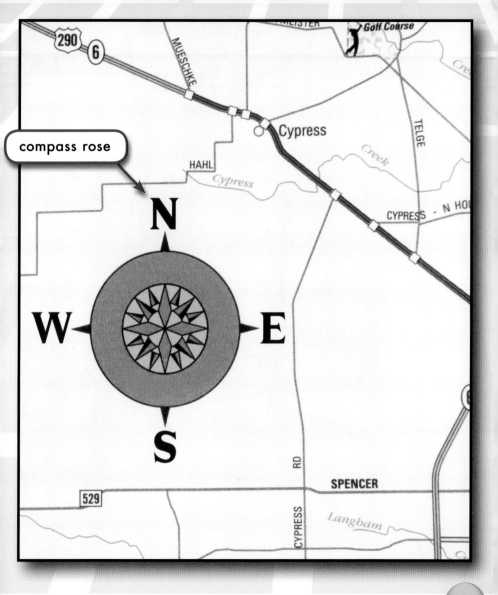

compass rose

North, south, east, and west aren't just points on a map. They are places on Earth. North on a map or globe points toward the North Pole.

13

Compasses

A compass shows
where north is on Earth.
A compass needle
always points
toward the North Pole.

Using Map Tools

You can use a compass and a map to travel. First, use the compass to find north on Earth.

Next, turn your map
so north on the compass rose
points to Earth's north.

Follow the map

to get where you're going!